Order this book online at www.trafford.com
or email orders@trafford.com

Most Trafford titles are also available at major online book retailers.

Print information available on the last page.

ISBN: 978-1-4120-2007-7 (sc)

Trafford rev. 02/25/2019

 www.trafford.com

North America & international
toll-free: 1 888 232 4444 (USA & Canada)
fax: 812 355 4082

About the Author

Vera Turner is a life-time educator specializing in learning skills that assist special needs students. She is an expert in teaching reading and learning techniques.

Until recently, she focused her teaching expertise in the Special Education classroom as well as regular preschool through college levels while developing the Keep-in Step techniques. She now shares this insight with the world in this book, on her web site (www.keep-in-step.com), during special consultations, lectures and workshops.

Currently, Vera lives on her ranch in New Mexico. She has three grown children, five grandchildren, and one great-grandchild who have all benefited from the Keep-in-Step routine.

She travels extensively sharing her Keep-in-Step Adventure with current and future friends she makes along the way. Her other interests include politics, bird watching, reading and archeology.

Table of Contents

Introduction
Keep-in-Step Adventure

Keep-in-Step is an adventure to make reading, learning, and other mental and physical activities easier. Reading and learning the ideas presented in this book are made easier by skipping to the 'HOW TO' section. The text is helpful to educators and active people using the technique. Use of the routine increases creativity, memory retrieval, attention span, learning, and coordination. The benefits of the Keep-in-Step technique will be quickly observable in many aspects of daily activity.

The benefits start immediately and attained levels of proficiency remain. Lengthy diagnosis time is unnecessary, since the technique works whether the source of the difficulty is known or unknown. The most dramatic results are demonstrated in folks that have minor blocks to learning. Severe special needs may require special directions and modifications as well as repeated use of the Keep-in-Step routine.

Successes of a diverse group of people with different interests and difficulties will be demonstrated in the case histories, also known as SUCCESS STORIES. This routine has been distilled from different fields of study including Sensory Motor Integration, especially with the trampoline, and Neuro-Linguistic Programming.

* * *

HOW TO

You need a distance of at least 20 paces to walk. Let your hands drop to your side. They should be empty and out of your pocket. It helps to shake them to be sure your fingers are relaxed. Look in the direction you will be walking, but don't zero in on a point. Look forward with a generalized focus being sure that you do not look at the floor or your feet. Walk letting your arms swing to and fro. This must be a relaxed walk with no muscle tightened.

If you are worrying about how you look or if you are putting too much thought into how you are supposed to do it, the routine will not work. Practice these two parts walking relaxed with arms swinging and maintaining a generalized focus in front of you.

The walk must be in a cross-pattern with the right hand forward as you step with the left foot. The left hand moves forward as the right foot takes a step. This is a problem for some folks, but is a natural walking pattern for most.

If this walking pattern isn't natural you may want to go to a 'toy soldier' step which is exaggerated. Extend the right arm as you step with the left foot and then extend the left arm as you step with the right foot. Keep the generalized focus away from you and add the rote language task out of rhythm (fast).

When this is going well, add language interference out of rhythm. Try the ABC's really fast or counting very fast. This must be a rote language task that doesn't require cognitive thought.

When you add the language interference, often times it will disrupt the walking or focus. Repeat until you can do all three parts

1. relaxed focus,

2. moderate rate of walking,

3. rapid rote language task out of rhythm with the walk.

Keep-in-Step, a routine developed by Vera, centers and allows the brain to function optimally. All learning is accomplished when the task becomes automatic. The transition from cognitive direction of an activity to automatic performance happens in an instant. Let the Keep-in-Step routine become a part of your daily life and watch your increased proficiency in all activities and learning.

Keep-in-Step allows the automatic system to show you what is known. Getting internal language and cognitive direction out of the way allows you to perform at your best whether you are on the golf course, sitting at the piano, or doing whatever you want to do better.

※ ※ ※

Keep-in-Step

The routine is simple; the results are overwhelming. The common response is, "Yes, improvement is noted, but I don't know how.

Over years of using the technique and observing the changes I can say unequivocally that the routine is responsible for subtle and dramatic integration that allows you to perform at levels you didn't know were possible.

The changes feel so natural and integrated that

the person doing the routine feels completely responsible for the improvements. And certainly the person did 'know' all of the integrated learning, because the routine does not teach a new skill. The knowingness was already present. The routine frees your system so all of your perception and performance is maximized.

On a simple level, we all know that negative self-talk can ruin a game or hinder performance. Another subtle inhibitor is tense muscles. Everyone has heard the old adage, "You are trying too hard. Loosen up."

An important part of doing the routine is to be sure that none of the body is rigid. When I observe a person doing the routine, I watch for any 'freezing out' or tightening of a muscle. Sometimes this is as subtle as holding the breath or a finger in a closed position. Sometimes a shoulder is raised. Often times a person will hold one or both arms stiff. So the instruction to allow the arms to move in a relaxed, alternating pattern provides a check on whether or not the person is 'freezing out' or tightening a muscle group. He may need to breathe naturally or shake his hands to loosen up.

The three parts of the Keep-in-Step routine are discussed in detail in the HOW TO section. First, you have a distant generalized focus, then you walk in a relaxed cross pattern, and last you add the rote language task out of rhythm. When the last part is added you will sometimes notice a change in the walking. Your arms may stop moving or out of balance movements may cause you to step or lean to the side or your eyes may dart to the ground or to a close focal point.

Perform this exercise until all three parts are coordinated. The muscles in the face and around your eyes begin to feel relaxed. After reading this, you may want to try the technique. Feel the relaxation, enjoy the broad distant focus, walk and talk. Once the routine is learned and performed in a relaxed manner the distance you walk is very short. I do it in my living room, but it is a lot more fun outside walking, talking and viewing nature with a generalized focus. For those of you that walk regularly, just include the routine in a small part of your walk. Be aware of what your eyes are focusing on as you walk. A distant, nonspecific focus and a balanced, relaxed body will give you maximum benefit for your walk. Hopefully, you are not carrying anything so both hands and both shoulders are relaxed. Use the rapid ABC's or number counting to add the language interference out of rhythm.

The benefits start immediately and attained levels of proficiency remain over time without practice. Learning to play a musical instrument demonstrates this aspect of the technique.

* * *

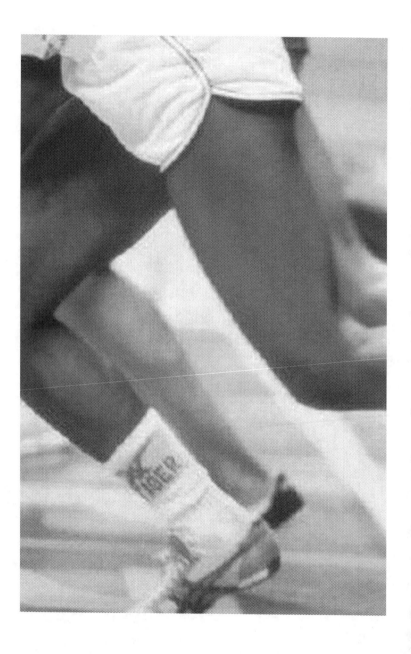

Keep-in-Step Template
(Tucker and Anita)

Traveling 43 miles to school each day with Anita, my riding partner, gave me lots of time to review the successes and diverse applications of the Keep-in-Step adventure. Anita heard all the ins and outs of the application. She is a mother and first used Keep-in-Step activity with Tucker, her son, who wanted to win the race during the field and track day at the end of the school year.

Each day, Anita and Tucker took a long walk to

the stock tank to be sure the horses had water. Anita used this time to teach Tucker all three parts of the technique which he exercised on the way to the tank. Then she suggested that Tucker run to the tank and back for track practice. She saw the immediate change in Tucker's stance and take off. Prior to his Keep-in-Step experience his body knew how to do the running, but the anxiety of a race had been holding him back on the take off and stiff running posture had slowed him down. After doing the routine, Tucker looked like a natural on the track and brought home some ribbons!

All my talking started making sense to Anita after she saw for herself the dramatic change in Tucker's running. The following months I was still talking about applications of the routine and pointed out to Anita that over a two month period her son had gained tremendous poise and when

I talked to his teacher she had noticed dramatic academic improvement in paragraph writing. The carryover from one activity to another as a result of using the routine is overwhelming.

Quietly one morning Anita asked, "Would the routine help me with my fiddle playing?"

"Sure, how long have you been playing?"

Anita continued telling me about practicing off and on for two years.

"What is your level of proficiency?" I asked.

Anita was able to describe how she worked at picking out a song. She was concerned about her timing so she liked to play with her mother accompanying her on the piano. I knew this would be a good test because even though Anita had practiced often she continued to have rhythm problems and stiffness while playing.

I described the manner in which she needed to do the routine as a test. First, play two pieces that are the most comfortable to play. Then, put the fiddle down and do the Keep-in-Step routine with the language interference out of rhythm.

Next, play the two pieces again and notice the difference. She continued to play and was amazed at the difference. She expected to have improvement in timing and tempo, but she wasn't prepared for the new fluid movement of the bow. The natural feel of the bow in her hand and how it glided over the fiddle strings shocked and pleased Anita.

Anita is a busy teacher so she put the fiddle away and didn't take it out for over three months, a perfect test for the long term benefits of the Keep-in-Step technique. I checked with Anita. Not only had the fiddle remained in its case, but Anita had not done the routine again. To test the long term benefits, I asked her not to do the routine. Just take out the fiddle and see if she had maintained the dramatic improvement in fiddle playing. She did this and was happy to report she was at the improved level with timing and use of the bow.

* * *

Benefits and carryover from Keep-in-Step

Integrated learning had taken place in an instant and Anita remembered her fiddle playing completely because of the total internalization of the task. The point of integration, when the skill becomes automatic, is the instant of real learning. Anita had been following directions, reading the music, and cognitively driving through the skill of playing the fiddle. Anita no longer had to do the cognitive direction of the task because she was playing the fiddle naturally.

In school, children sometimes have to cognitively direct the reading process. Reading becomes a laborious task of recall, sound blending of letters, and construction of phrases. Hopefully the brain can comprehend the meaning in between the struggling effort to read. The Keep-in-Step routine facilitates learning to read by integrating the skills so they become automatic, eliminating the cognitive direction. When you have to think through the steps of a process, the cognitive part of your brain is actually directing activities that need to be done automatically. When the automatic system is functioning optimally, you will soon notice the increase in creativity, awareness, and the fluid movement of your actions.

As a teacher I saw that this routine helped to eliminate the lengthy drills that take the fun out of learning. Integrated skills such as reading, paragraph and story writing are quickly enhanced by the Keep-in-Step exercise.

The success story of Tucker and his racing techniques demonstrates the carryover after doing the routine. Tucker wanted to win a race on track and field day. He did win some ribbons because, after doing the routine, he didn't stiffen and resist during competition. He ran with grace and ease. The carryover was noted by his teacher when his organization and paragraph writing improved.

Tucker was an awkward third grader who kept his head tipped down and when he was looking at something his body would follow. He was and is friendly, intelligent and interested in many subjects. About six weeks after he did the routine, I took a double take when I saw him. He had developed such poise. He was still friendly, intelligent and interested in conversation, and his body maintained a natural stance instead of following a faulty eye movement pattern. He engaged me in conversation with a very relaxed, poised expression.

Poise, calmness, and a centered feeling come from doing the Keep-in-Step routine. The noise pollution and hustle and bustle of life can get you out of sorts. To regain a calm, centered feeling and integration with the world around you try the routine and notice the difference.

Are you a person who uses Yoga, Tai-Chi, or meditation to gain the balanced, centered feeling? Do the routine and you should gain increased benefit from your program.

* * *

Development
of Keep-in-Step

The development of the Keep-in-Step routine has been an adventure and has evolved through years of working with children and adults in the classroom. Early in my teaching career I learned the importance of eye movement in learning to read. Studies show that training eye movement produces improved reading performance. Auditory and visual perception training helps a student to focus and increases learning ability. We each have a personal preference as to how we learn depending on whether we are predominantly auditory, visual, or kinesthetic learners.

Sometimes one channel used for taking in information is distorted and doesn't work as well as it should. Think of yourself; you probably prefer to see, or hear, or touch whatever you are learning. So often you will say, "Show me how to do that. Or tell me again how that happened." Or you may stand up and get in the big middle of what needs to be done.

My interest and specialty is HOW we learn. Early in my teaching career I observed perceptual intake of information and concentrated on visual perception as identified by Marianne Frostig, a pioneer in the study of visual and auditory perception. In 1975, I became aware of what Jane Ayres was doing with integrated movement and perception. She developed and published an inventory test of Sensory

Motor Integration that was used by the Sacramento Crippled Children society.

A class, called Learning Styles and Channels, gave me the first clue regarding how to add language interference when doing the integrated movement. The idea was not taught in the class, but when I was describing the techniques I used with my students the assistant instructor just said, "Try adding the ABC's out of rhythm." I did and observed the speed with which students were integrating the learning.

While teaching preschool I observed the correlation between motor skills and language development. I worked with many special needs students who carried various labels. Teaching reading through the 1980's also showed me how much movement effects language and the reading task. Following are a few examples of how I arrived at my understandings.

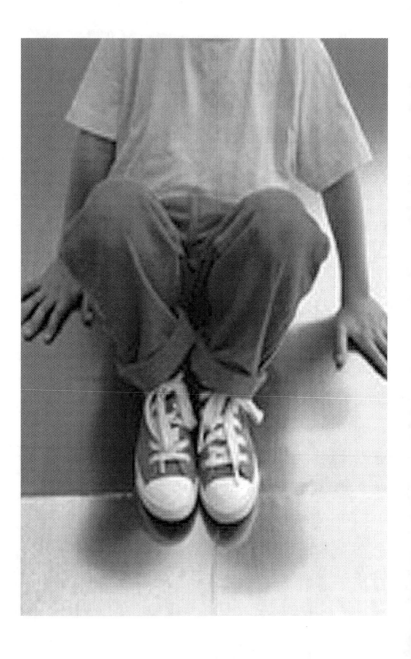

Mark's Success Story

Mark was a second grader at the Turner Ranch School. I sent Mark to be tested at the Crippled Children Center in Sacramento, California. His disabilities were not severe enough for the Jane Ayres' program, but they gave him a number of exercises for me to do with him. His dominant channel of learning was auditory. He liked to listen to learn information so that was the stimulus I was supposed to use to train his eye movement and to teach new skills. He was in second grade and wanted to jump rope. He couldn't jump in, so I told him to close his eyes and listen to the rope, and when it hits the ground, JUMP IN. He did it once and from then on he could consistently do it! I had called his auditory perception to the foreground and then he could perform the task. I wish I had known my Keep-in-Step exercise to integrate the entire movement, but that came later.

Jimmy's Success Story

As Title I Reading Teacher, I was called to observe a kindergarten student. The teacher was concerned because he would not talk. He would listen to lessons and on occasion responded with one word answers. He seemed to be attentive and his classroom work showed that he was intelligent.

I worked with Jimmy and noticed he walked as if he were on ice and he was afraid to step on the jump-board---a laminated board resting on two low saw horses. He looked at the ground and would not talk to me at all.

After two weeks of diligently working with Jimmy, he learned an even jump with natural arm movement and no stamping as his feet hit the board. The feet must allow a fluid spring into the next jump. Jimmy had started by holding my hand just to step on the jump-board. He was frightened and held his arms stiff as he came down hard on the board without any spring.

I had asked his teacher to let me know when he started talking, because I had already noticed the dramatic expressive language development that came from guided trampoline activities. The morning after Jimmy mastered a smooth rhythmic jump, his teacher met me at the door all excited,

"Jimmy started talking. He just came in talking. Talking in complete sentences."

Jimmy helped me to learn about the two week time table. It takes about two weeks for language to emerge. What I didn't know at the time was the importance of the language interference out of rhythm. Luckily, I naturally chattered encouragement to Jimmy as he struggled to coordinate the jump and arm movements. I also used touch as an anchor. When Jimmy first started on the jumpboard, he grasped my fingers as an anchor to balance while standing and starting to jump. If the student doesn't know the ABC's or how to count, it is almost as effective to chatter while he is doing the jumping or walking. I always asked Jimmy to look at me and I would position myself in front of him. Now, I get quicker results with the distant generalized focus.

Language development, writing organization

and fluency are affected by the Keep-in-Step integrated movement and more dramatically when you add language interference. It took about two weeks to get the coordinated rhythmic pattern to Jimmy's jumping, but when he mastered it language emerged! With this timeframe in mind I started predicting the point at which language would emerge.

A Six-Year-Old's Success Story

The summer of 1997, I was introduced to a six-year-old girl who had an interference in her language development. At age two, traumas had bombarded this child and she started using her own language. She had ideas and knew what she was saying. She could speak English words, as shown by her 'polly parroting' the last two words of what was said to her.

If you said, "You have a pretty blue dress."

She would repeat, "Blue dress."

If she wanted hot chocolate, she would point to the cupboard that held the cups and say 'RED'. Red had little to do with what she wanted, but the family learned what she was trying to say.

The adults would quickly give suggestions and try to second guess what she was talking about. They were good at interpreting her language and motions. I asked them to allow a three second processing time delay before expecting her verbal response. When she was excited and wanted to say something quickly she would lapse into her own language. Before the Sensory Motor Integration training on the trampoline she was developing her own language with English sounding syllables, but she used her own intonation and construction. It was a fast, free flowing language and she seemed to know what she was saying. Her own language only entered when she got agitated and eager to express something from her memory. She couldn't relate events that had happened earlier and she couldn't relate feelings.

I observed the child, grandparents, and parents interacting. I like to observe in the child's natural setting, if possible. She was taking swimming lessons in her Grandma's pool. Swimming, an excellent cross patterned activity, was giving her extreme difficulty. Her hands were thrashing—windmill fashion.

This child had lots of advantages provided by the parents. She had finished a fast track language/thinking/processing computer program and was receiving speech therapy through the University of California, Davis. The speech therapist was concentrating on noun vocabulary. This six-year-old was speaking in two word commands and not using the 'to be' verb at all. She was very flighty and her eye movement was the same. The parents had heard of the advantages of the trampoline, so when I suggested getting one they did so immediately. My prediction was, "If this is going to help, she will be speaking in sentences in two weeks."

I worked with her on the trampoline. At first she would 'freeze out' the arm movement and 'bang' with two feet together and throw her body forward when she came down. With lots of instruction, she started letting her hands go up when she went up. Then she would land and rebound with a spring like jump. She was not able to include the language interference, but I was putting in nursery rhymes and counting. Her movements would get out of rhythm as soon as I started talking. I would coach her back to the rhythm of jumping with 'big arms' in the pattern. Again, I would use language interference and within the two weeks she was able to maintain the rhythm with some language distraction. In two weeks, almost to the hour, she came into her Grandma's house and responded to the question, "How was school?" with a complete sentence describing an action that had taken place at school. Relating an event from her memory had been an impossible task just two weeks before.

I was with her for just a few weeks in the summer, but before I left she had started using appropriate English language. This student needed a concentrated program because of the severity of the disability, but natural language was started and her own language that she was developing slowed. In 1997, when I worked with this six-year-old, I still believed the trampoline was essential to the process. The trampoline and eye movement techniques are powerful in cementing certain learning, but not essential.

Kate's Success Story

I would like to relate another complicated case history that proved to me the power in the Keep-in-Step exercise. I had been using the trampoline and other complicated integration activities, but this case taught me how to use the Keep-in-Step routine.

Kate was 14-years-old at the time we started working together, and was having trouble learning in her special school. I talked to the Director of the school and she asked if what I did was invasive and did it involve medication? When I answered no to both issues, she was interested.

The only information I had before meeting the child was that she had been labeled with 'Failure to Thrive Syndrome'. When I met her, she had a strange rolling 'get-a-long' to her walk. I asked the Director if this was her normal gait and 'Yes' was her answer.

The child didn't speak in sentences, instead she gave one and two word responses followed by an embarrassed laugh and then she would duck her head. I had a trampoline to use while working with Kate. I worked for 45 minutes trying to teach her how to jump with a coordinated movement. Her arms needed to move in a pattern and rhythm before I could introduce the language interference. Her feet needed to meet the trampoline without banging and when done correctly the rebound would be smooth and she would go higher and higher.

This 'Failure to Thrive' case was not working. She was distracted by others in the yard. She would start to jump, then she would 'freeze out' parts of her body and stop the rhythmic movement. I was exhausted and thought I had found a student that would not be able to benefit from my sensory motor integration activities. She had very erratic eye movement and I had difficulty getting her to focus on anything.

When Kate got off the trampoline, I stepped back to think of a way to reach this child. I checked her eye movement which was about the same as a three-year-old. I moved to an open area and using a stick I drew a line in the powdery dirt. I asked Kate to just walk toward me using the line as a target. She as unbalanced as the preschoolers years ago had been on the balance beam. I was pulling from all my past experience with sensory motor integration so with Kate's teacher beside her I taught teacher and student to do a stiff toy soldier type cross pattern walk. They walked about ten times back and forth just to learn to make these movements. You could see the conscious thought going into each movement. I also used touch to let her know which foot and which hand to move. This helped Kate to maintain the distant focus while learning the cross patterned walk.

First in slow motion, and then she mastered the movement and maintained the distant focus. The teacher added the language task out of rhythm. Kate was able to do the coordinated pattern while teacher and I did the language interference. Finally, she was able to maintain the automatic task of walking (still kind of stiff but it was cross patterned) and talking at the same time.

She did this forward and back twice while looking at a target.

We had been working for over an hour so we were both tired, but I told her to go to the trampoline and do her jumping. She got onto the trampoline. She drew a deep breath and I said, "Go ahead. Do the jumping the way I showed you. Keep it going."

She jumped about five times coordinated with natural arm movement and a graceful rebound. On the fifth time, she realized how terrific she was doing and she stopped, sat down, laughing hysterically, and almost crying with pleasure.

I just told her, "You will never forget, never forget. You will never forget how to do that. Great! Super! That was perfect."

All of this took place in the Director's yard and others had arrived so we stopped our lesson. The real thrill came when I observed Kate walk from the house to the driveway in a perfectly natural cross-patterned walk with normal posture. The Director looked at me and I asked, "Did you see that?"

Her expression and response was as if she had witnessed a miracle.

I had been doing the integration exercises on a jump-board or trampoline, but this case showed me a step-back from the trampoline work. It is so simple to do, but so dramatic in its results. Certainly it is not invasive and doesn't have any ill side effects.

* * *

The simple exercise that I share with you in the HOW TO section is a synthesis of patterns of movement that I have used for 30 years working with students from preschool to adults. I have observed the benefits and the connection between movement and language performance.

With Kate the Keep-in-Step routine was born and the result was Kate could perform the motor skill that I had been trying in vain to teach. The Keep-in-Step technique works as effectively to teach a motor task as it does to teach a language skill.

* * *

Motor Skills and
Keep-in-Step

Working with Kate I realized the impact of this simple routine and how it would apply to motor tasks. I began to explore the motor skill application of the walking and talking. I used the routine on myself when I tried to learn a karate step. This was certainly a new activity for me and I could feel the difference before and after. This new revelation sent me on a quest to test all possible applications.

Soon, I knew it would benefit any learning situation including skiing, golfing, learning to play a musical instrument, recovering from a stroke, and overcoming depression. Success stories I described above are cases where I saw the difference. Recognizing the broader applications of the Keep-in-Step technique prompted me to first put up a web page, then hold a workshop, and now to write a book.

Erik, the avid skier testimonial, is on the web page and it demonstrates the benefit of getting cognitive thought out of the way so you can perform at a maximum level of proficiency in a sport.

* * *

Erik's Success Story

Erik is a competent skier and in the last few years he challenged himself to the task of learning to telemark ski. He had been diligently practicing with his telemark friends, a small group of skiers. Telemark skiing is so much more difficult than alpine skiing that there were only a few hundred in the world.

Erik described his progress to me, "I'm having trouble on the turn to the right. I do the left turn okay and occasionally I do the right turn perfectly. Naturally, conditions of the snow make a big difference. But I just wish I could get the right turn as good as I can do the left."

I told him about the application of the Keep-in-Step sensory motor integration exercise. I had just realized after working with Kate that this routine could alter the performance of a motor task. I described in detail the three steps. All of my instruction was over the phone because Erik wanted to try the Keep-in-Step technique next time he went skiing.

After his big day I got the report. Erik did the routine before he went up the hill. He just told his buddies, "I have to do this and I'll tell you about it later."

He proceeded to do what he called his <u>RAIN-MAN</u> counting. Erik spent the day at the top of the mountain mainly doing traverse skiing instead of downhill so he really didn't notice a difference. I am not sure if he did the three parts completely. If he was too worried about how he looked in front of his friends, the routine would not be allowed to work fully. He would not get full benefit from the routine if he didn't completely shut down the internal language that was telling him that he looked silly or this is stupid and won't work. At noon Erik came down and actually stretched out because his back was hurting.

After lunch Erik had a more private chance to do his <u>RAINMAN</u> counting as he called it. He repeated the routine because he had not noticed any difference during the morning. That afternoon at the top of the mountain he didn't truly test the right turn that he had identified as the critical attribute that needed improvement. At the end of the day, he decided to go straight down the hill with the Left and Right Telemark

Turns. He did so and was thrilled on the first run. He felt like a natural. His body was doing the execution of the perfect turns and he was able to note the difference in the stance that relieved his back. The hurting back was actually a manifestation of an improper stance on the Right Turn. This was a powerful response to my telephone communication of the Keep-in-Step adventure.

Erik finished his tremendous success story with the words I often hear, "I'm not sure if it was the <u>RAINMAN</u> counting that did it."

"I am," I confidently responded.

* * *

Sometimes it is easier for an outsider to observe your improvement because it just feels so natural to you. Read on and you will be as confident as I am in the power of Keep-in-Step.

If you want to test the routine, you need to find a skill that you are learning. Hopefully, it is something new to you. Do your task and then the routine before performing the new task again. If you have coordinated all three parts of Keep-in-Step, then you will notice a marked improvement.

Have fun with the Keep-in-Step adventure---my grandsons do. I shared the technique with Scotty and Steven in California. At their ages (9-10) they were learning new information and motor skills every day. They had watched their Dad do the routine before golfing to give himself an edge on the golf course. The next year Steven, my younger grandson, was the starting pitcher for his Little League team. He remembered the activity, so he did his walking and talking before the game. Afterwards, he was eager to tell me about the shut out inning in his first game and he was the winning pitcher!

Big brother interrupted his story to say, "Oh, yeah, but he did his walking and talking before the game." He interrupted with the comment as if his brother had cheated by doing the Keep-in-Step routine before his game.

Big brother Scotty was showing me his new talent on the violin. He was missing a few notes in each piece, but I was proud of his efforts. I asked if he would like to get the benefit of two hours of violin practice. He said, "I don't ever have time to practice that much."

"Then do your walking and talking, because that's like practicing for hours. Just do it and tell me the difference you feel."

He knows how to Keep-in-Step with a relaxed cross-pattern walk, looking at the far end of the room, and he quickly recited the ABC's. He walked 20 paces back and forth two times. I was not sure if he had done enough to gain the benefit, but he picked up the violin and played a piece without any error.

"That was great. Could you feel the difference?"

He just shook his head, indicating yes, and kept playing without a mistake. My grandsons have learned the benefit of walking and talking. They can feel the difference and you, too, may have a shut out inning, if you use it. It is not cheating. It feels so natural and yet it gives you such an advantage.

How Often?
How Far?
Why Even Do It?

The answers are as diverse as the people who set out on the Keep-in-Step adventure. Specific results in one skill requires as little as twenty paces. I usually have the person repeat the twenty paces three or four times. The repetition gives him or her a chance to completely relax without 'freezing out' certain muscles, and to add the language interference out of rhythm while maintaining a generalized distant focus. Specific skill improvements have been checked weeks later to be sure the participant maintained the level of competence achieved.

At times, repeated use is necessary especially if there is brain injury or surgery. Sometimes a complicated learning disability is present and repeated use of the Keep-in-Step routine is necessary.

The lengthy use of the Keep-in-Step technique is usually associated with brain injury or surgery. Stroke recovery and long term depression also take repeated use of the process. Severe learning disabilities require repeated use as well as intervention in the relearning process.

* * *

Internalized Learning and Learning Disabilities

You have truly learned a task when you can do it automatically. Learning to read is the major task for students in our school system. Some aspects of learning to read include learning phonics, memorizing words, practicing for fluency, and exercising eye/hand coordination. Most teachers just assume students comprehend---this assumption is just tested rather than taught. Students have learned to read when the whole process is raised to an automatic level so they are free to comprehend. When reading automatically, you do not continue to sound out words. Instead, you will read in phrases and concepts which become remembered mental pictures.

The same is true with writing. When you are thinking, using cognitive thought, to construct the sentence, the product is stiff and doesn't flow. To reach fluency in writing takes lots of practice. But even with extreme amounts of practice you won't get very far if you are just practicing error. The sensory motor integration exercise separates the cognitive and the automatic functions and frees up what the automatic system already knows.

The Keep-in-Step exercise will not teach you to play the piano if you have never tried. Thinking through how to do something is ok when you start to learn, but it gets in the way of the natural performance. You will notice improvement when you get the language and cognitive thought out of the way so that you can perform the activity naturally.

* * *

John's on the
Job Success Story

John had undergone brain surgery for a tumor a few years before. He had trouble with short term and long term memory. Memory problems made it difficult to carry out his duties as a store clerk. John is a friendly, caring, diligent, young man making his way in the world. John changed jobs to a more demanding sorting and filing job where accuracy and speed were important. John was so well liked in the community that townspeople were rooting for his success. The job was so demanding that complaints were coming in daily due to mixups and just plain mistakes. John's boss knew that a decision had to be made, but before she would terminate him she came to me.

"Do you think that thing you did with Tucker and Anita would help?" June asked.

"Sure, and it certainly can't hurt."

I went to the office while John was not present. I taught June the subtleties of doing the routine and I told her what to expect. Knowing that John had undergone brain surgery, I mentioned that he would need to perform the Keep-in-Step routine each morning to clear the pathways.

June showed John what she had learned and suggested that practicing Keep-in-Step might help him sort faster and more accurately. He did the routine and experienced his first day with only one minor misplaced article. John's astounding, increased accuracy with the sorting task occurred after one Keep-in-Step exercise. June felt like she had witnessed a miracle since she had been straightening out the confused filing and delivery that John had been doing for weeks.

John continued to do the routine and continued his excellent performance. June encouraged the walking and talking over a six week period. The dramatic improvement after implementing the routine allowed the fellow to keep his job. When he stopped the Keep-in-Step routine, his performance would drop back to unacceptable and complaints started coming in. June suggested that they do the routine again and he was back on the improved job performance.

By using the Keep-in-Step exercise John had learned his job. That which normally takes weeks to learn had been accomplished in the intervening months. John had totally internalized the learning associated with performing the new job. In about three months he had mastered the job to the point where he recognized the errors of others. That is when he made the comment, "I'm not any different. Everybody has to learn the job."

About two years later I received word that John regressed to his original level of performance. John never recognized and acknowledged the importance of the Keep-in-Step process in his learning of the job, which is not uncommon.

After six weeks of disintegration of job performance, June had suggested to him that they once again practice the Keep-In-Step exercise together. She reminded him that doing the routine had increased his sorting and filing accuracy two years ago. He refused her suggestion and offered other excuses for his mix-ups. He told June that he "just needed to focus more" not realizing that the Keep-in-Step routine allowed him to focus immediately.

The origin of the resistance to such a simple technique is not clear. It is possible that some resistance is due to the individuals lack of awareness of the Keep-in-Step's successful impact on all aspects of the their task performance development. The learning skill advancement is so subtle and natural that the Keep-in-Step process is not acknowledged by the student as the source of their progress.

The Keep-in-Step technique cannot hurt, so give it a try.

* * *

Severe special needs usually require special directions and modifications as well as repeated use of the Keep-in-Step routine, as noted in John's on the job success story. The technique was born out of the frustration of trying Sensory Motor

Integration techniques while using the trampoline with Kate who was carrying around a label of 'Failure to Thrive Syndrome'. One reason for the necessity of extended, use of the routine is the troubling task of unlearning mistaken skills.

I have worked with children and adults who have had brain or spinal surgery. Most of them have been in or recently dismissed from rehabilitation programs. Keep-in-Step integration exercise added to their program enhanced everything they were doing.

Often times the changes are so subtle you won't realize that Keep-in-Step is responsible for the observable improvements. Maybe you were going to have the tremendous gain in performance at this moment anyway. Often times you have already witnessed the improvement in tiny flashes so you now recognize the feeling continuously. The routine permanently sets the learning so it is a 'normal' level of performance instead of brief glimpses of this higher level of mastery.

Long term difficulties have another system working to hold you back. An emotional filtering system of the brain is in charge of protecting you. Every perception, thought, or analysis of any situation is filtered through this system to be sure it is not going to hurt you. If you have failed at a task so many times, you may get a message to the automatic system that says, "shut down, don't try, this person is belittling or being mean to me, poor me, I CAN'T."

Everyone has experienced these negative messages and each person has their own method of dealing with them. If you could do a simple exercise to quiet this input, think of the freedom you would have to perform at the highest level of your true ability.

Brandon's Success Story

Brandon's success story illustrates the process of unlearning and correcting known tasks. Brandon came out of six years in special education where he was grouped with retarded students. His math concepts and computation were at beginning first grade level and reading was at a weak third grade level with many bad habits. He was intimidated just by the teacher looking his way and became especially defensive if the teacher tried any individual instruction. Brandon's writing was illegible and the construction of a sentence was almost impossible. His oral language was so rapid and choppy that it was difficult to follow his thinking.

Using the Keep-in-Step exercises during Brandon's sixth grade year, he gained about three years in math and brought his reading level up to a strong fifth grade. Through Writers' Workshop his writing became coherent and a passion with him. He continued over the summer to write books. The unlearning and relearning of the academic subjects was an arduous process with emotional stumbling blocks from years of failure. Brandon did the Keep-in-Step routine often and was able to accomplish the unlearning and redirecting that allowed him to make these gains.

Basketball was his new task so he had no unlearning to do. When you saw him on the court he moved with the grace and poise of a professional. Because there was no unlearning that had to take place, his performance was completely natural.

During the summer he continued writing. Composition was also a new skill and just separating the writing from the failed tasks of spelling and letter construction allowed Brandon to enjoy and master the task. Brandon displayed dyslexic tendencies and had been classified as learning disabled. The years in special education had handicapped him. He was intelligent, outgoing, and liked everything to move fast. After a year of using the Keep-in-Step exercise and participating with a normal class, Brandon was on his way to succeed in life.

* * *

Todd's Success Story
(*Learning Fears*)

The year before Brandon entered my class, I had learned a lot about the Keep-in-Step routine and how fear and old negative reactions to learning can be eliminated. Todd and Leo, my grandsons, came to live with me during their seventh and sixth grade year respectively. Todd, the seventh grader, had not learned to read and his math skills were behind because he was getting extra help in reading during Math time. I was able to work in all aspects of his life, since he was my grandson. I had the boys at home but also I was their teacher because I taught in a little school where sixth, seventh, and eighth grades were together. They couldn't get away from Grandma/Teacher.

I was familiar with Todd's family and academic problems. After being in Special Education for a few years he was behind in Math which was his strong subject. He had not made many gains in reading. He could read some words, but he would not for fear of failure and because he couldn't read a book that looked like a seventh grade level.

In school, when I tried to help him with his math, he would become defiant and resisted anything I said. I stopped trying to teach. I told him that nothing I said could help him when he put up such a resistance. I talked to him at home when he was not feeling threatened and ask, "Do you want to learn the math?"

He ducked his head and said, "Yes."

I talked to him for a long time about how he felt when I tried to work with him on a specific problem. He began to recognize his resistive stance. I told him that he cannot learn when he puts up that shield. It is physically impossible for the brain to take in any information during that state.

At school, I didn't even try to teach him when he developed that attitude but I did let him know what he was doing. As soon as Todd had truly identified that feeling and was able to identify the triggers that caused him to feel that way, he was able to do what I call a 'mental swish' with those feelings. I asked him to bring in that feeling at a quiet time at home and to push it away replacing it with the receptive feeling of wanting to learn. As soon as he could image the resistance with the strong feeling that goes with it and acknowledge the relaxed, inquiring feeling that he wanted to put in its place, I asked him to do it mentally five times very fast. By the fifth time it was almost impossible to bring in that negative, resistive feeling. He was a different student after that day.

Another time this feeling came into play was when he had his picture taken. He would freeze into this terrified feeling and his picture reflected the look of a frightened traumatized teenager. Again he did the 'mental swish' with that traumatic feeling and replaced it with a relaxed, unthreatened feeling and from then on Todd was very photogenic. This control allows any person to feel better about themselves. I think of this process when people talk about empowering others.

With this heightened feeling of self worth, I approached the subject of his reading. Todd had been sitting with his book open and not reading anything. He thought I didn't know. He had worked on comprehension skills and spelling. He had never had 100% on a spelling test until he used Keep-in-Step to enhance his learning capabilities.

I tested Todd with the first grade inventory of letters, sounds and sound blending. He didn't know the vowel sounds, but he did know the consonant sounds. He knew the letter names so the long vowels were easy. He learned quickly the vowel rules and the vowel combinations. He was able to sound blend, but more importantly he knew how to swish the feeling of panic away when he met a word he didn't know. As soon as he got rid of the feeling of panic, he started reading. He was thrilled with this new skill.

The other hurdle he had to overcome was being called on in the classroom. Todd would act out and most teachers would just throw him out of class. At home we could talk about this feeling and before he returned to Arizona with his family he did respond in class.

When his mother enrolled him in the Arizona school, she gave them his background of Special Education and the accomplishment of the six months with his Grandma in New Mexico. The new school tested him and he was reading just one year below grade level. Todd's mother advised the new teachers that he had been a non-reader the year before. Todd was integrated into the classroom, but still had Special Education assistance. I felt honored to have had the time to work with my own Grandson. He felt a little silly, but he jumped on the trampoline saying the ABC's out of rhythm. He did the swish with the unwanted feelings that he had identified. I still had not realized that the trampoline was not essential to the changes.

Lexus' Success Story

I have worked with Lexus as a tutor and a friend. In first grade she was having numerous learning problems with reading, spelling, handwriting and math. Her eye movement was very scattered. Her eyes would dart from, here to there. I worked only one time with her eye movement but over a two month period she had continued school and did the Keep-in-Step exercise at home once or twice a week when she walked with her Mom.

Two months later Lexus came running up to me with a confident posture and showed me her journal and said, "I came up five levels in reading." (These are intermediate steps, not grade levels.)

Her handwriting had improved significantly and she was so happy about her 100% in spelling. I noticed her confident look and I asked her to follow a target to check her eye movement. Was this just developmental? Did she practice eye movement or handwriting? No, but this is where she showed how much she had integrated with the Keep-in-Step exercises. I had shown her only once how to remember the spelling words, but she did it for each word on the new list.

* * *

The panic associated with being asked to read in front of others and the sheer horror at not knowing how to perform an activity will stop learning. The panic will also stop performance even if the skill is known. This phenomenon can be observed during a sporting event if a player gets distracted by negative thoughts. Classroom teachers often observe students experiencing learning blockage. You may have experienced the feeling when you were in school or even now anytime you are required to take a test. Test taking anxiety is so common and so debilitating that it deserves a section of its own. Amber had been plagued with test anxiety most of her life and the following story shows how she took control of the fear.

Test Taking Anxiety
Amber and Jake's Success Story

Amber was nervous and pacing the floor the night before her State Boards. She had completed the course in nail and facial technology. She was good at it, but test taking was not her strong point. On the trampoline, she did the swish to replace the nervous pretest jitters with confidence and the ability to calmly focus on the content of the test.

To do the swish, she had to recall the panic that she felt each time a test was put in front of her. I used the motion of placing a blank piece of typing paper in front of her representing the confrontation of a test. I recreated this action to intensify the emotional feeling of panic connected to test taking.

Amber also had to remember a time when she felt completely confident and capable. She has a natural ability to train horses and she was able to bring in the feeling of confidence that she experiences when she starts working with a horse.

As soon as Amber could image the test jitter feeling and also the pure confident feeling she felt as a horse trainer, she was then ready to do the swish. I asked her to bring in the bad image. She then pushed the bad feeling to a pin point in the horizon and brought in the good feeling to replace it. This has to be done five times fast. It needs to be done with no direction since it must be done quickly and without interference. By the fourth or fifth time it was almost impossible for Amber to bring in the bad feeling. She had replaced it with the capable feeling and went in the next day with her new found confidence and passed the State Board Exam on the first attempt.

After her own successful history using Keep-in-Step, years later, Amber was very pleased and receptive when I offered to help her son Jake. He was having trouble in school and stuttering. Most of his problem was behavioral and the school wanted to use drugs to calm him down. He was active and inattentive at times. Amber did not believe he had Attention Deficit Disorder (ADD) which school personnel had labeled him. At times, in a classroom, he would get over stimulated and tune out but the behavior was not consistent. No behavior was consistent, not even the stuttering.

Some times it would be really bad and other times it would almost disappear. Jake is very bright and his academic skills are good. He loves to read and spends long periods of time just reading.

In November of 2002, I worked with Jake a short time with the Keep-in-Step technique. He was very resistive, stiff and throwing his body instead of just walking. He reached a fairly coordinated walk after many attempts and I was helping him with language interference. He only did it halfway, once, so very little improvement took place. His neighbor had a trampoline, so I showed him how to find a focus point when he was jumping and asked him to count really fast. I also showed him the difference between a hard landing and a soft cushioned landing that would allow him to spring up again.

Amber took Jake to a Psychologist that used biofeedback technology to measure brain wave patterns. Early in the treatments, the doctor said that Jake did not demonstrate any pattern of classic Attention Deficit Hyperactive Disorder (ADHD). He did have some extremely notable problems with one side of the brain returning to a sleep state rather than staying at attention. This would explain how Jake would literally tune out while you were talking to him.

During Jake's sessions with the biofeedback doctor he seemed to show improvement, but it was not consistent. One week there was a big improvement in his speech. It was so dramatic that Amber and the doctor noticed that the stuttering had almost disappeared. Guess what? This was the week that Amber had gotten a trampoline for the family. Jake had spent many hours on the trampoline and he must have been doing some of the focus and chattering while jumping. Jake began to extremely dislike attending the biofeedback sessions, so Amber stopped the treatment. Jake continued to jump on the trampoline, however bad weather and his realization that his Mom wanted him to jump soon ended this routine. Jake's stuttering had diminished and his teachers could understand his speech more clearly but it was still better or worse at different times.

During the summer of 2003, I worked with Jake again on the trampoline and he was coming down too hard and not getting a high spring out of his jump. I showed him how to go higher and higher using his arms and making a softer landing. He humored me by doing the distant focus and using the language interference. I also had him find two focus points and while jumping he would follow my directions as to which one to look at. His stuttering improved and the family only occasionally noticed a regression into stuttering. This was a marked improvement that his teachers noticed when he returned to school. I worked with the whole family and this made homework easier for each of them.

White-out and Swish

Amber used the swish in conjunction with the Keep-in-Step idea on the trampoline to get over her test anxiety. Later you will read how Fred used the white-out process along with the Keep-in-Step technique to drastically reduce the amount of time that he experienced depression.

White-out and swish are two techniques that I learned from a friend and he referred me to the book <u>Using Your Brain for a Change</u> written by Richard Bandler. These two processes reflect the immediate impact of Neuro-Linguistic Programming. No one else is programming you. To do the process you decide what you want to get rid of and what you want to replace it with.

Personally I used white-out and the mental swish to stop smoking. I had used every method except alternative nicotine supply. I smoked off and on for 49 years quitting for nine months to two years a number of times. Each time I would go back to smoking and each time I quit I gained and lost ten to twenty pounds. It has been six years since I quit the last time using the trampoline and the white-out process followed by the mental swish and the Keep-in-Step routine. I concurrently used the white-out process with the food cravings that often follow quitting, so this was the only time I didn't have a big weight gain associated with quitting smoking. This is a technique that can be used for compulsions, addictions, test anxiety and panic.

Todd used the mental swish to correct poor learning habits and to get rid of the panic he felt when he met a word he didn't know. He also replaced the recoiling fear when he posed for a picture with a calm confident feeling.

You have probably said about dieting or a bad habit, "Oh, it is just a mind set. I can do it when I make up my mind."

The mental swish and the white-out along with the Keep-in-Step technique are ways to create a determined mind set. When you are in the grasp of a compulsion you are just doing the swish in reverse.

This was so clear as I was listening to TV and a lady described her fears. She was afraid to go out of the house because she might be hurt and die. She didn't want to get in a car, plane or train for fear she might be killed. She was worried that her young husband might also be killed. She was literally making pictures of these scenarios and bringing them in close and making the pictures vivid with lots of feeling and breathing in the horror scenes. Her body was reacting to the fear stimulus as if the pictures were happening. There was no room in her mind to bring in a calm, peaceful picture.

To eliminate fears, compulsions, or bad habits you must vividly picture in a mental snapshot and internally feel the problem. Then visualize where you want to be and how you want to feel. In the white-out process you dump the negative picture and feeling onto the white (paper, wall or object) and look away from the white as you breathe in the calm, relaxed picture of yourself free of the addiction, compulsion, or fear. Walk through this once slowly to be sure you have the sequence correct being careful to dump the negative picture and breathe in the positive, calm feeling and image. As soon as you know how to do the process, perform the white-out technique three to five times fast. If you are doing it correctly it will be impossible to bring up the old negative feeling.

The swish is very similar and almost as powerful.

You can do it anywhere without a prop. The lady on TV was doing this in reverse so she would get stuck in panic mode. If you are quitting smoking or any other strong habit, you know how the feeling to drop back into the habit just hits you. So when the draw toward the habit happens, acknowledge it and bring in a picture of you and the bad feeling. Bring that picture very close and powerful on your mental screen, then push the picture to a vanishing point. Immediately, from that point, bring in your familiar calm relaxed picture of freedom from the habit. As you push the picture into the distance, you will notice the reduction in negative feelings so it is an easy transition to the positive freedom associated with the positive picture.

If you are taking the time to do the mental swish or white-out, please do the simple Keep-in-Step routine. The sensory motor integration of the

Keep-in-Step technique sets the learning of the new habit. Soon the trigger feelings that sent you toward the bad habit will trigger the positive sense of freedom and you will find yourself drawing a deep, relaxed breath.

It has been over six years since I smoked, but on occasion I still have the trigger feeling that makes me think of a cigarette. The feeling has diminished and now it quickly moves to the picture of freedom from the habit and I still take a deep breath, almost a sigh of relief that I am free.

Years ago I used the white-out technique with a student I was tutoring. He had a compulsive habit of sucking on a glass. He would do this repeatedly until his mouth was a huge circle of red and chapped and his lower face was all rough and red. Other kids in his fifth grade class made fun of him, his parents spanked him, his teacher scolded him and still he continued.

One day I asked him, "Do you know what causes your mouth to be all red?"

He answered, "Yes." He continued to tell me what he did to make it red.

I asked, "Would you like to stop sucking on the glass so your face could heal?"

He wanted to have a normal face and to stop others from teasing him so I had him think about how it would look to have a smooth, clear face. Also how would it feel to look at classmates without being teased. Then I asked him to think about the feeling he had just before he put the glass to his mouth. With a white sheet of paper I had him do the white-out process. He dumped the compulsive desire to suck on the glass and replaced it with the relaxed feeling and a clear face. He did it three times fast and he was able to stop this terrible habit. It took a few days to heal, but teachers, parents and the young boy were thrilled with his new control. The kids had nothing to tease him about and he didn't feel agitated so he could better concentrate on his studies.

Remember how Todd used these techniques to get rid of the panic associated with reading and to rid himself of the resistance to learning associated with years of failure. Test anxiety is quickly relieved using the swish and extremely helpful when taking tests.

Breakthrough Learning

Stories of breakthrough learning have come my way and I just have to remind myself that it doesn't matter who gets the credit for the accomplishments. The person who achieves the learning gains the reward.

At church there was a family that had just

bought a trampoline for their kids. Both boys were ropers in the rodeo circuit. I talked to their father for a long time about how to use the trampoline to increase proficiency with roping. I didn't even mention the carryover to academic performance. This is a situation where I just had to share the Keep-in-Step process.

"Just get the jumping going with arms going up as the body goes up, and say the ABC's out of rhythm. Oh, and be sure to look ahead into the horizon."

It was a year later when I heard the mother talking about the breakthrough in learning. She gave his teachers all the credit for reaching this kid and how he had turned on to learning. I did remind her that she had provided the trampoline and that it's use is a big part in the integration of learning. It is not important for the kids to know where the integration came from, rather it is important to the kids that it happened!

Once a child has felt the difference in processing and learning after doing the walking and talking they will do it for themselves. For instance, Steven, my grandson, did it before his game. Also, I had a student after Christmas vacation say, "Mrs. Turner, will you do that walking 'thing' with me. My head is all mixed up."

During my public school years, I did lots of Keep-in-Step activity on the playground during my endless hours of yard duty. I would show interest in the students at the jungle gym. They would perform tricks and skills on the equipment enabling me to observe their coordination challenges. This provided an opportunity for me to give directions for skill development that fit into what I knew about the Keep-in-Step process.

Chin-ups really helped to balance the focus and I talked to students about the distant focus in relation to the balanced use of the muscles. Sometimes they would perform a coordinated pattern of walking or jumping. I would do chattering language interference and then ask them to say the ABC's out of rhythm. I was not always privy to the gains that they made, but I often heard from their teachers that the students had matured and made tremendous growth in academics. This gain was no coincidence---Keep-in-Step was working. I was happy for the children and delighted that other teachers acknowledged their growth. I also knew these students had been introduced to a technique that would help them integrate learning for life.

* * *

Fred's Success Story
(Depression)

Adults that have experienced the difference will try it again to reach another plateau of performance or accomplishment. Fred, a friend of a friend, listened to me expound about the Keep-in-Step routine and the applications. Fred, a builder and businessman, is quiet, intelligent and very perceptive. Summer of 2002 Fred described the bipolar condition that he suffered with in terms of % of time in HI, LOW, or optimal functioning time. He is very aware of the time that he is in each level. When I find a person who has a quantitative account of the problems they face, I sure like for them to do the Keep-in-Step technique and give me feedback on the results. Out in the yard on the continental divide near Pie Town, New Mexico, Fred did the infamous walking and talking exercise. I was on my way to California for a few months and didn't get any feed back until November, three months later. Fred reported significant increase in the length of time he was in the higher productive level.

The following Spring, Fred was talking about the improvements and thinks it may have been the Keep-in-Step exercise that allowed it. "I need to get back to doing that," was Fred's comment.

One evening I visited with Fred and he was busy jumping on the trampoline. I took my turn jumping as I shared my trampoline applications of the Keep-in-Step process and talked about the combination with the white-out technique. The white-out process is similar to the swish in that you bring in the desired outcome.

This is the technique I used to stop smoking over five years earlier and it is the only process that was successful.

Fred has fewer periods of depression and they are shorter in duration now that he has done the white-out process on the trampoline. He described the depression as much more manageable since he could move through it easier and quicker. After using this technique Fred is able to identify the triggers that bring on the depression which makes it easier to avoid it all together.

* * *

Depression debilitates to the point of not being able to get started. Organization and productivity are gone. Depression interferes with sleep, job performance and all of life's pleasures. Bipolar condition wavers between depression, manic state, and normal production. These conditions improve by use of the Keep-in-Step routine. Any exercise or program is the last thing a depressed person will initiate on their own. The beauty of the Keep-in-Step routine is the tremendous result from short performance. By the time you show a depressed person how to do it and you ask them to show you that they know how to do it, the benefits will start. Severe depression requires repeated use hopefully on a daily basis. For people that are aware of the changes, this is incentive to continue the practice. But inertia takes over and depressed people put it aside like most New Year's Resolutions.

* * *

Josh's Success Story

Every day I meet people that seriously need to use the Keep-in-Step routine for a wide variety of concerns. Usually, Keep-in-Step enters the conversation when a person relates a terrible predicament.

My friend's grandson received notification that he was not going to graduate with his class. Many injustices in the system had led to this problem, but Josh was having trouble with math and needed an 80% on a particular test to pass the course.

After intense work with his tutor he did not pass with the 80%.

I contacted the grandmother and asked if Josh's mother would call me. After a lengthy conversation with Josh's mother, I met with Josh. He was not allowed to graduate with his class, but a few days later he was allowed to retake the test to receive his diploma. My meeting with Josh was five days before the test. This is not time enough to master the course so I worked with test anxiety. He learned the swish technique to image the test anxiety and push it to a distant point and breathe in the confident feeling and posture that he wanted to maintain. Everyone who knew Josh noticed the difference in his posture and demeanor. He now projected a sense of confidence.

Josh had to remember a number of formulas which were essential for passing the math test. There was one formula that he thought he knew, so I asked him to bring it to his visual screen. I asked, "Can you see the formula."

"No," was the response after straining to see something in his head. "But I can write it."

Josh wrote out the formula but when we checked later there was an error in the formula.

Since Josh was not in the habit of visualizing specific items that he needed to remember, I showed him how to put words and formulas on his internal screen. He did this and was able to visually manipulate the items. At first, I had him put known words onto his screen and then change their color. He also would bring them in close and push them back, change colors again, and change from print to cursive. When he could visually manipulate items on his internal screen, I had him look at the correct formula written in red and transfer it to his internal screen. He was able to do this quickly and then change color and push it back and forth. Josh will never forget that formula and now he has a specific technique for remembering.

Next, Josh did the Keep-in-Step routine to set the learning of these new learning techniques. We had only worked with one formula so most of what he was learning was 'how to learn'. Josh had only five days of Keep-in-Step practice before the test. He passed with an 88% and received his diploma after graduation. Josh's mother had a graduation party for him and he received many cards and letters of congratulations from friends and his extended family. Josh cried with joy and his Grandmother and Great-Aunt noticed Josh's confident posture.

Later I wanted to hear how many changes his family noticed. Patrick, his dad, reported the noticeable difference in Josh's attitude and confidence. Patrick also did the Keep-in-Step exercise and tried it with his classmate in his Jujitsu class. A lady in Patrick's Jujitsu class was having trouble with a move involving her left side. She did the Keep-in-Step routine and noticed immediate improvements.

* * *

This is a routine that can be applied many places and on the spur of the moment. Pass on the information and maybe you will be able to improve the life of someone else.

Charlotte's Success Story

Charlotte, a friend of mine, played the guitar for Easter Sunrise Service. I talked to her before the performance and learned that guitar playing was new toCharlotte. She was nervous about performing so I related the Keep-in-Step routine and suggested that she try it. She was surprised when I said we could do it on the spot. We walked into the forest away from the campfire and crowd. She did the routine saying the ABC's out loud as she walked. I was impressed with her natural performance. She didn't look like a new player and didn't seem nervous at all.

Six weeks later I ran into Charlotte and asked if she had used the routine again. As a matter of fact, she had just used it at the rodeo when she was waiting to be called for her turn to rope. She was sitting on her horse so she had to modify the routine by pretending she was walking and doing the other two parts. She found a distant focus and audibly counted very fast. She really felt that it helped her to relax before her roping.

I am sure it did and I told her that I have used the routine with wheelchair bound people and others with severe limp or ambulatory problems.

Ken and Leo's Success Stories

Kate's mother referred Ken to me. Ken had surgery on his neck and it had left him with limited control of his left side. His muscles on the left side began to atrophy. Ken did lots of body building and worked diligently at getting better. He made one trip to the Occupational Therapist (O.T.) who showed him how to stand. When he finished his appointment, I asked him to do a white-out process to blank out the old posture and replace it with the new alignment. This along with the Keep-in-Step routine allowed the new alignment to feel natural.

This case prompted me to make arrangements for Todd's brother, Leo, to participate in the same program. His posture was so bad that he had difficulty in his weight lifting class. His muscles were so tight that he couldn't do the squats or touch his toes. When he lifted weights over his head, the weight fell down because of the severe curve in his upper back. This summer he changed that problem. The Occupational Therapist showed him how to stand and stretch crucial muscles enabling him to stand straight. Certain specific exercises helped him strengthen his back to hold a straight posture.

He has spent years slumped over, so he used the Keep-in-Step exercise to allow his brain to internalize the new posture and allow it to become natural. He enjoys seeing himself standing straight. Hopefully, the new posture will relieve the constant stomach trouble that he has been dealing with for the last few years. The hunched, curved body is not conducive to normal workings of the internal organs.

Leo is a teenager and all teens are concerned about their appearance. This has given Leo the incentive to put in the effort necessary for this tremendous change. Telling himself to stand up straight was not enough. When he tried to assume a straight stance, it felt like he was stretched in an awkward position. The talented O.T. relieved the old posture which allowed Leo to touch his toes for the first time in his life. With the application of the retraining technique of Keep-in-Step, her work was internalized and became a natural part of Leo. He enjoyed the new talent of touching his toes and being able to lift weight over his head and also the three inches in height that he gained by standing straight. Maybe now they won't call him 'Little Jensen'.

Leo used the white-out and swish techniques to get rid of the old body alignment and replaced it with the straight posture. The new posture has to feel natural or he would not be able to change, but remember Kate and her changed posture and walking pattern just from doing the Keep-in-Step routine.

How Can Keep-in-Step Help You?

After reading all these stories, hopefully you have thought of some ways that the Keep-in-Step technique will help you. There are so many applications for Keep-in-Step you can only benefit if you just do it. Don't worry about how it helps, just rest assured that your brain and body will do the learning. The Keep-in-Step adventure will increase creativity and sharpen your awareness. Enjoy the benefits! Remember, the results are so natural you will probably not give the routine the credit, but who cares. Enjoy your new freedom.

Acknowledgments

I am grateful to all the people that are profiled in this book and all who contributed to the understanding of the Keep-in-Step process which enhances learning. I would like to especially acknowledge the Datil Writers' Group without whose encouragement and valuable input this book would still be just an idea. I would also like to extend many thanks to Karen Reis, Patti Ziegler and Carol Pittman for their diligent reading and editing of this manuscript.